ODD ONE OUT

Buster Books

Edited by Helen Brown
and Lauren Farnsworth
Designed by Derrian Bradder

First published in Great Britain in 2018 by Buster Books, an imprint of
Michael O'Mara Books Limited, 9 Lion Yard, Tremadoc Road, London SW4 7NQ

W www.busterbooks.co.uk F Buster Children's Books T @BusterBooks

ISBN: 978-1-78055-581-2

2 4 6 8 10 9 7 5 3 1

This book was printed in May 2018 by
Leo Paper Products Ltd, Heshan Astros Printing Limited,
Xuantan Temple Industrial Zone, Gulao Town, Heshan City, Guangdong Province, China.

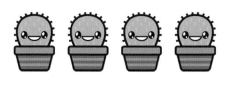

How to use this book

Simply pick a puzzle and follow the instruction on the left-hand page. Whether you're finding an odd one out, matching pairs or spotting specific emoticons, there's plenty to keep your brain bamboozled on every page, along with fun facts to keep you entertained. If you get stuck, all the answers are at the back of the book.

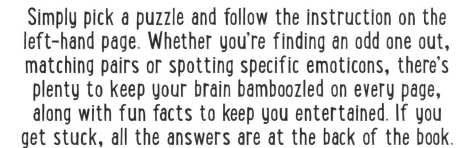

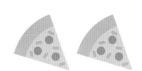

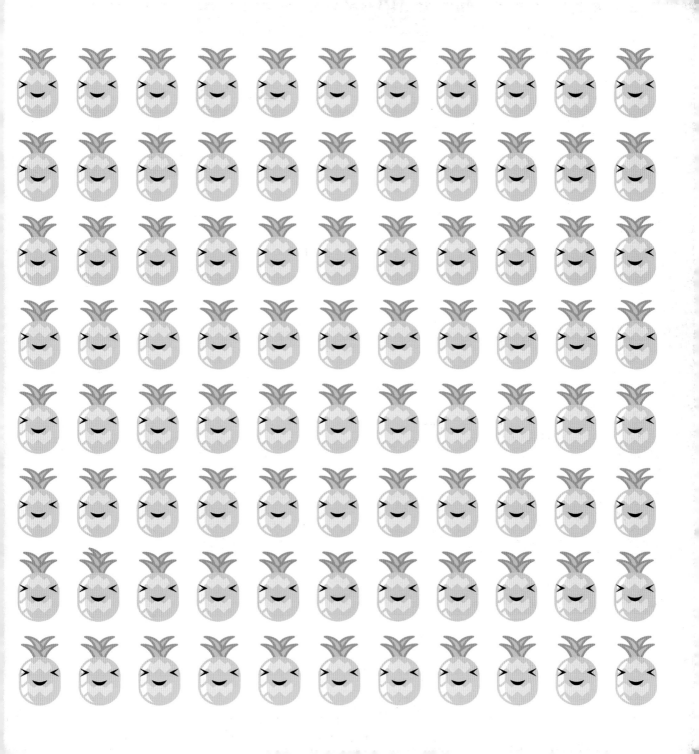

Which unicorn is the smallest?

The first known depiction of a unicorn was found in the Lascaux Caves in modern-day France. It is estimated to be up to 20,000 years old.

Spot the odd
one out.

Mesopotamian nobles built ice houses along the
Euphrates River at least 4,000 years ago, so
they could have iced desserts on hand. But ice
lollies and ice pops are barely 100 years old.

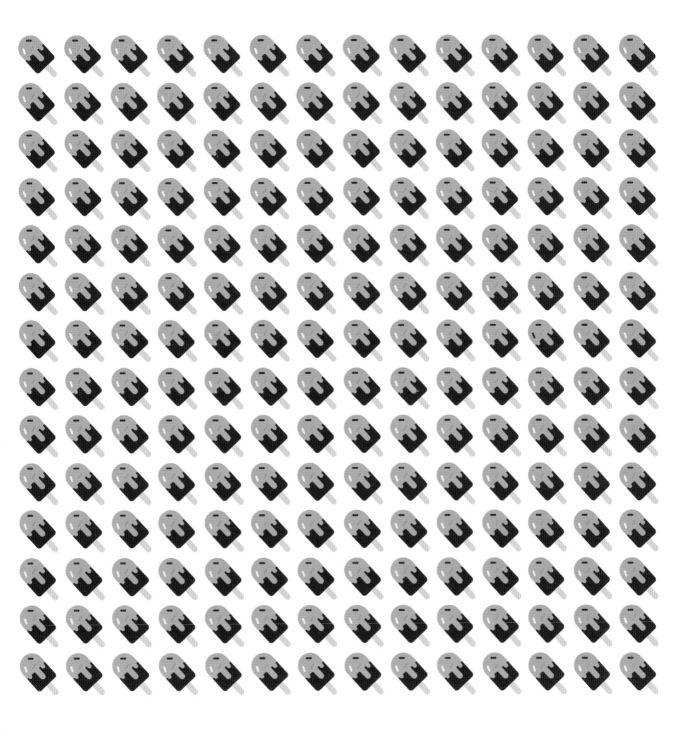

Find these four faces:

The tiger is the largest species of the cat family.

Find two odd pairs.

The spines of cacti can be used in the production of hooks, combs and needles.

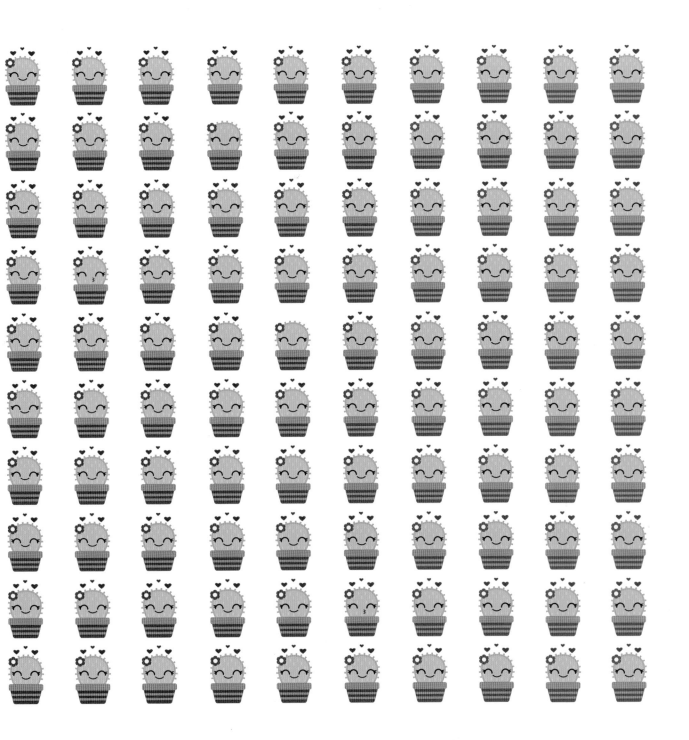

Find these six cupcakes:

Before sophisticated decorating equipment came along, people used feathers to spread icing on cakes.

Find one odd pair.

Apples are a 'pomaceous' fruit because the plant that they grow on flowers. The flowers on an apple tree are pink or white.

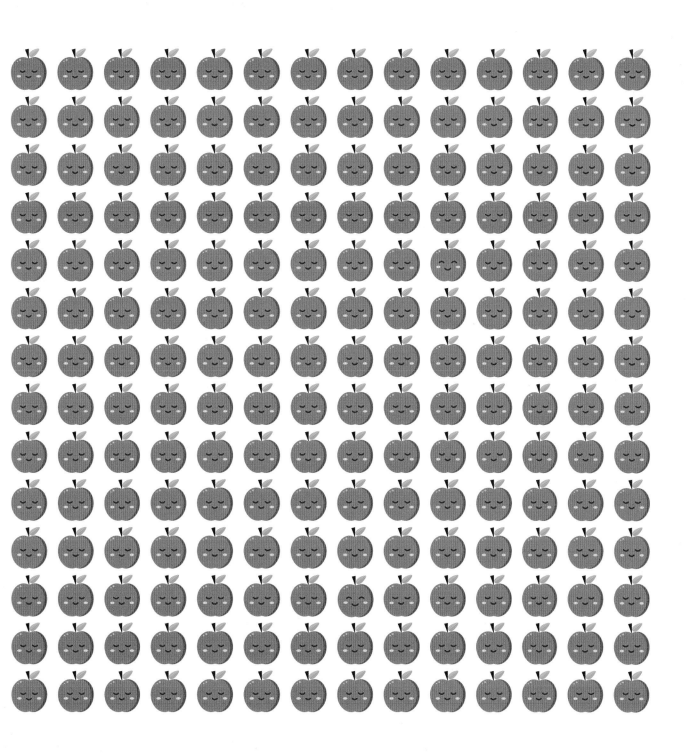

Which plant is the largest?

Researchers have found that plants can recognize family and will compete less for root space with their plant family members than when surrounded by plants that are different.

Spot two odd ones out.

The only taste humans are born craving is sugar.

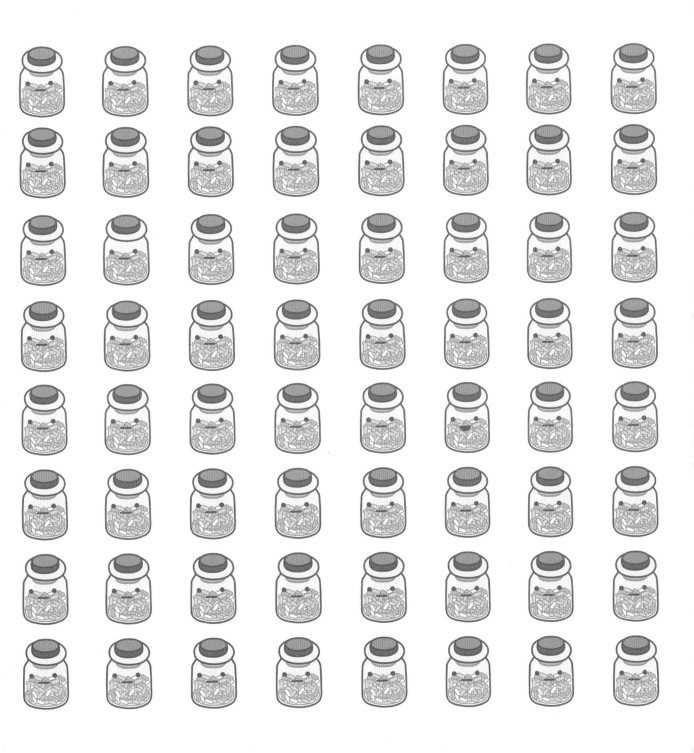

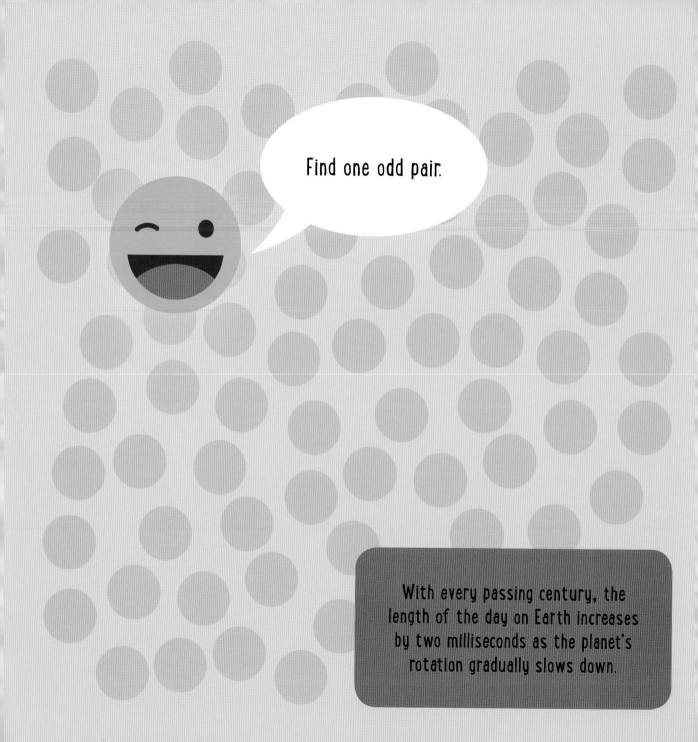

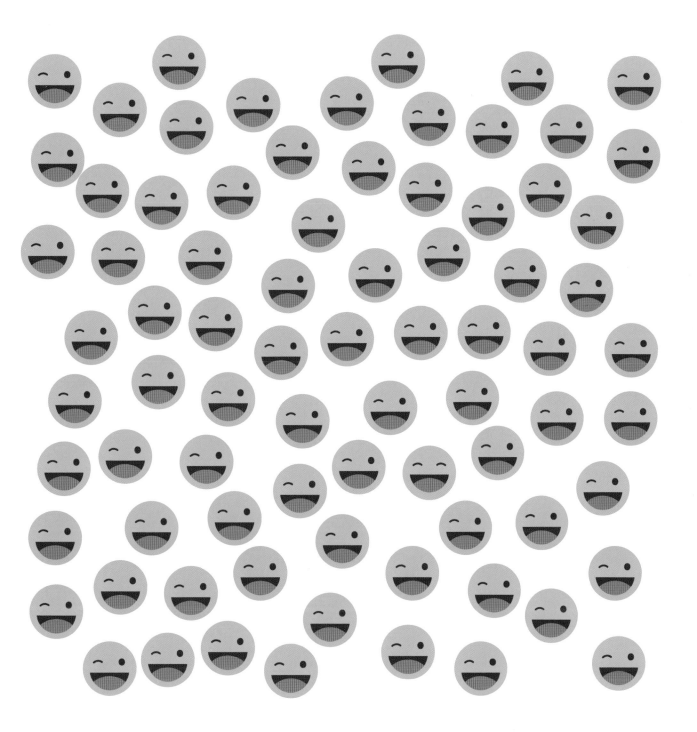

Find this face:

It has been suggested that the same part of the brain is responsible for both crying and laughing, perhaps explaining why they sometimes occur together.

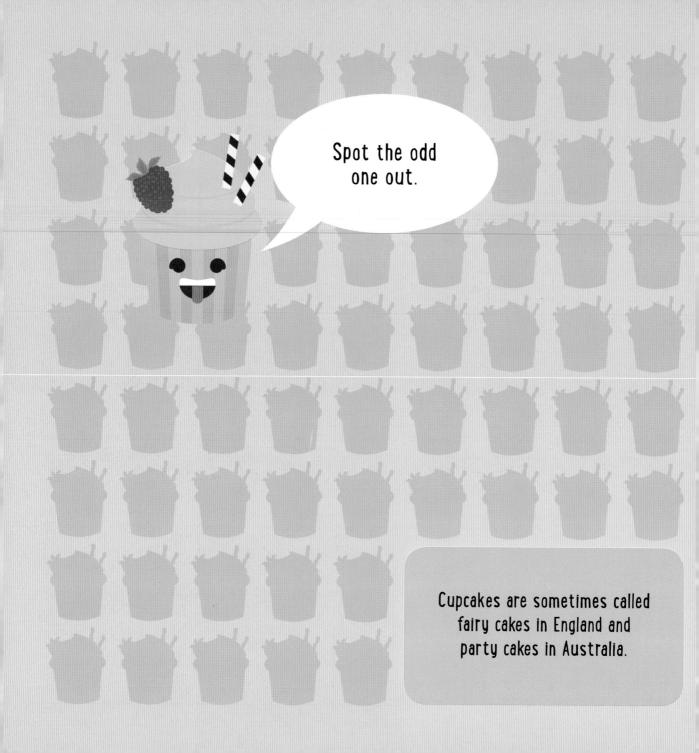

How many odd
ones out?

In its one-year lifespan,
a single seven-spot ladybird can
eat more than 5,000 aphids.

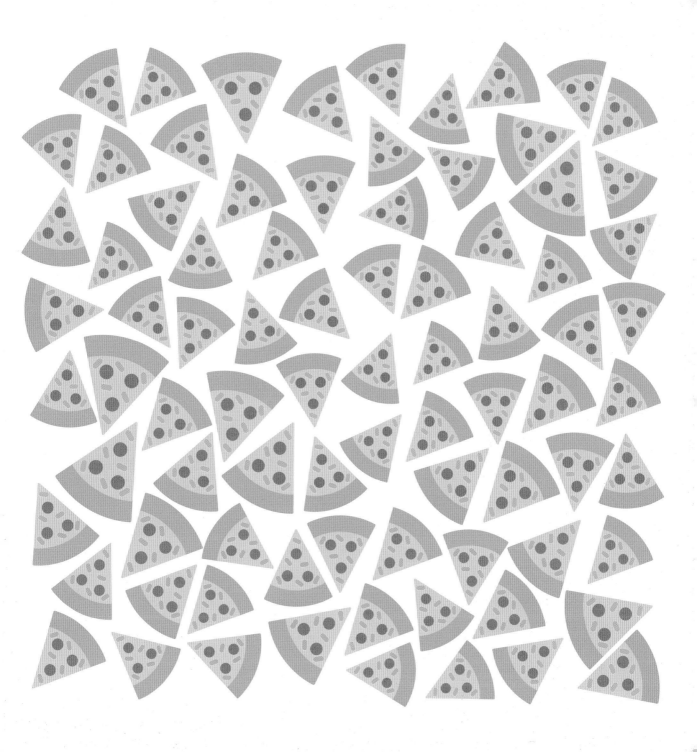

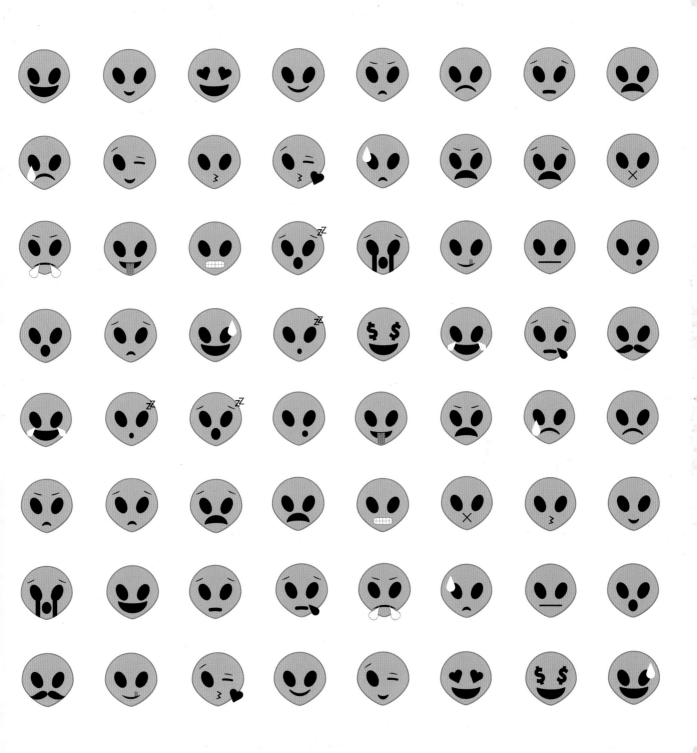

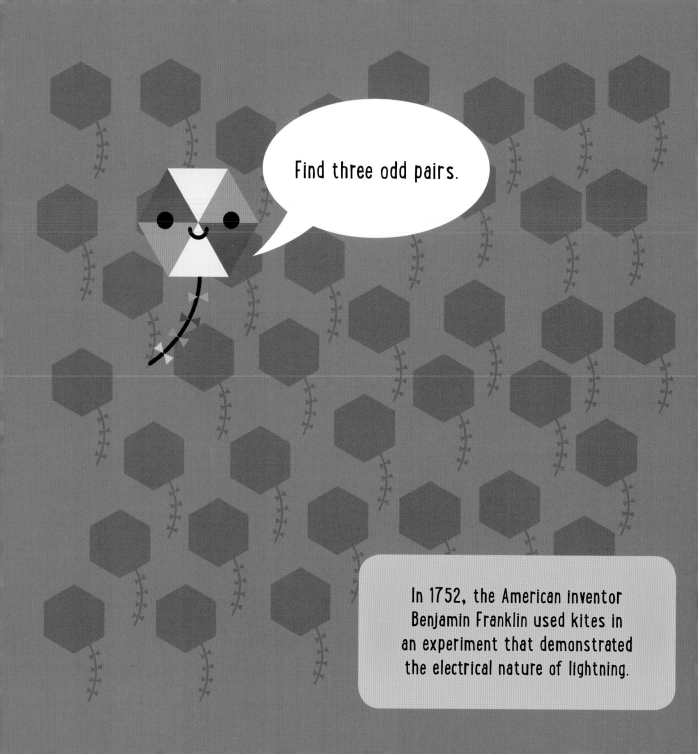

In 1752, the American inventor Benjamin Franklin used kites in an experiment that demonstrated the electrical nature of lightning.

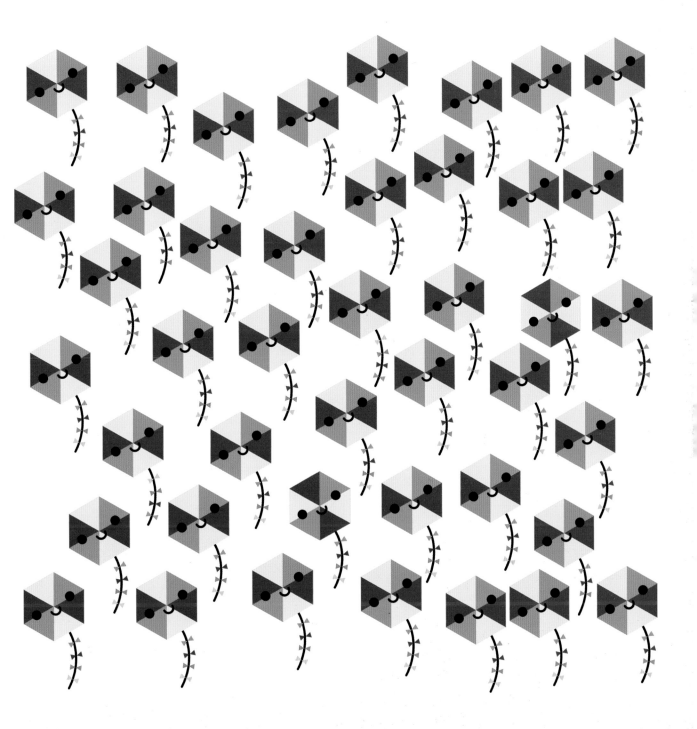

Researchers have found that simply being told you are blushing, even when you're not, is enough to make you blush.

Find four odd
ones out.

Dogs can recognize over 150 words.

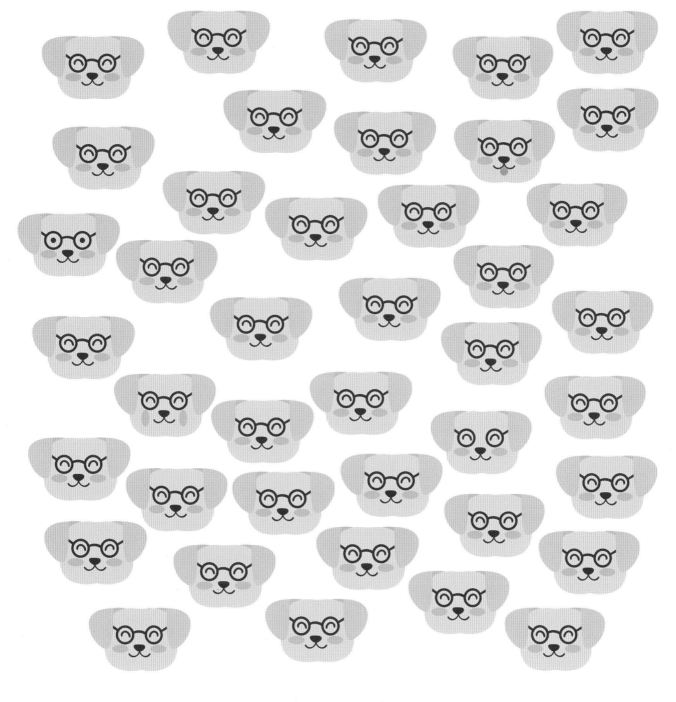

How many odd
ones out?

As of 2011, 13 people in the USA
have the first name 'Donut',
making it the 245,396ᵗʰ most
popular name in the country.

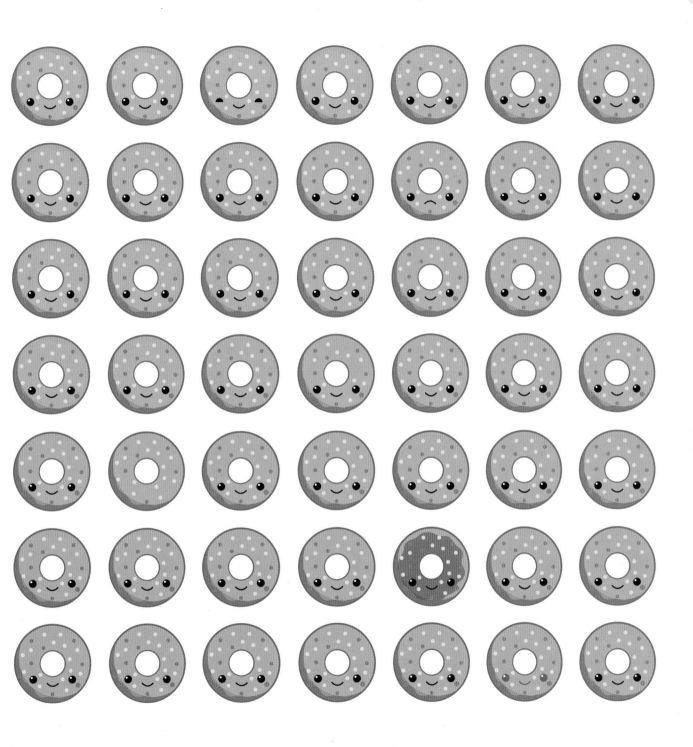

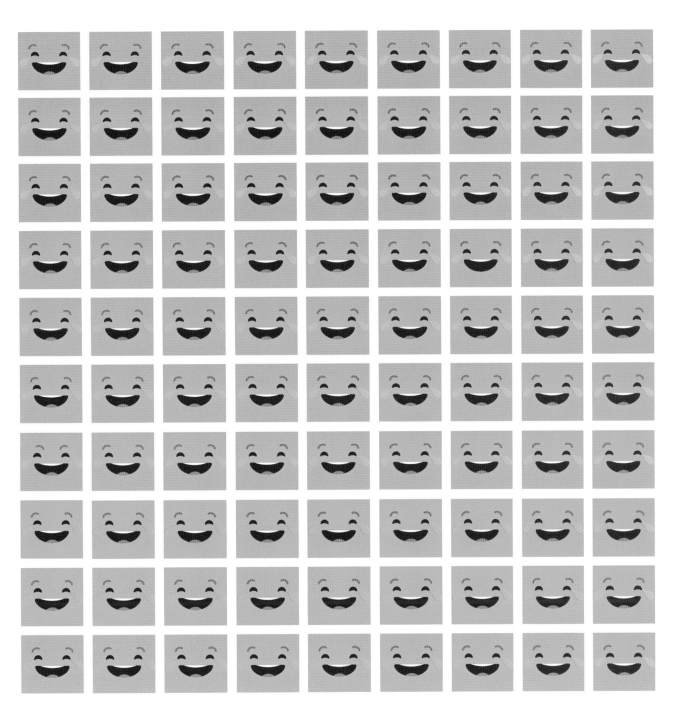

Find three odd pairs.

The smell of real Christmas trees came eighth in a survey of people's favourite smells, just behind the sea but ahead of perfume.

How many odd
ones out?

Saturn's rings span up to 282,000km,
but are amazingly thin at only 1km
or less in thickness.

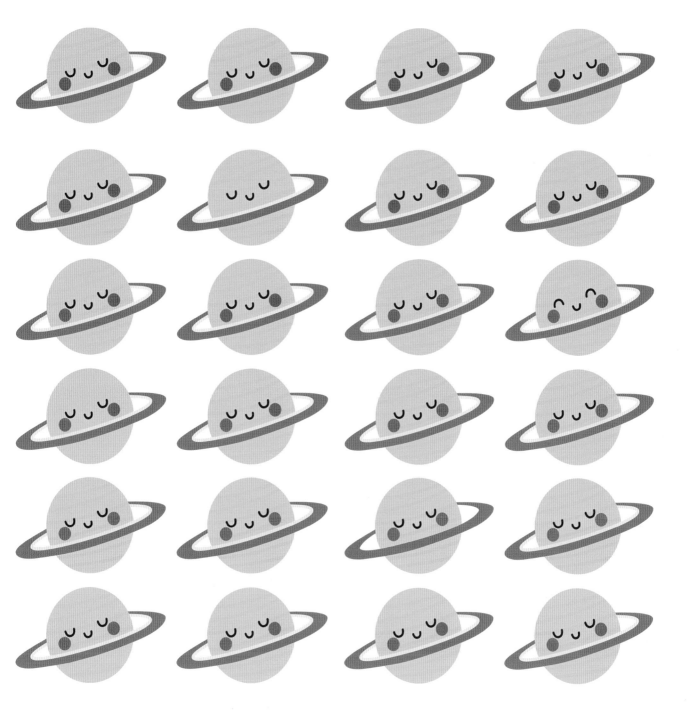

Spot six odd ones out.

When an earthquake shook the village of Yamakoshi in Japan, a Shiba Inu dog named Mari moved her puppies to a safe place. Mari then rescued her elderly owner who had been trapped beneath a bookcase.

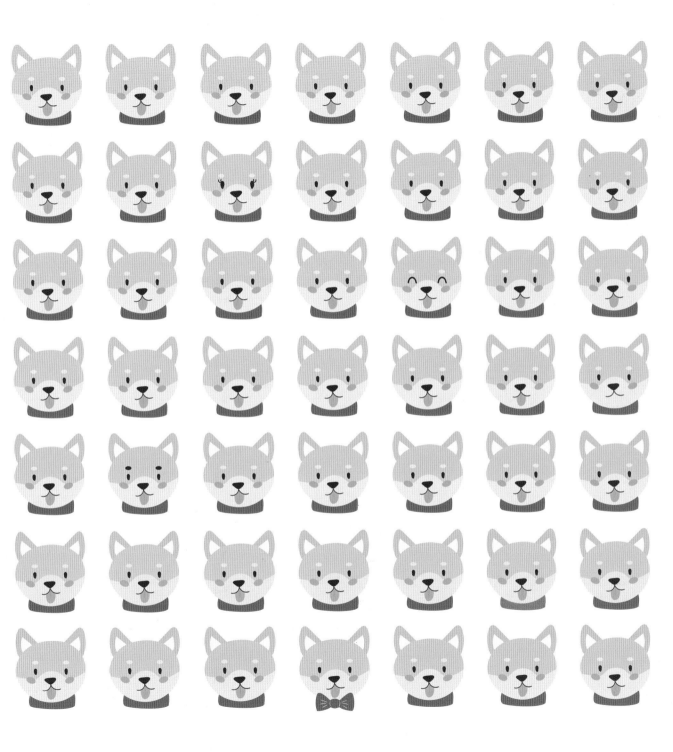

Spot five odd ones out.

Depending on the species, cacti can survive for 15 to 300 years.

Spot three odd ones out.

World Zombie Day was born in Pittsburgh's Monroeville mall in 2006, the location of George Romero's film *Dawn of the Dead*.

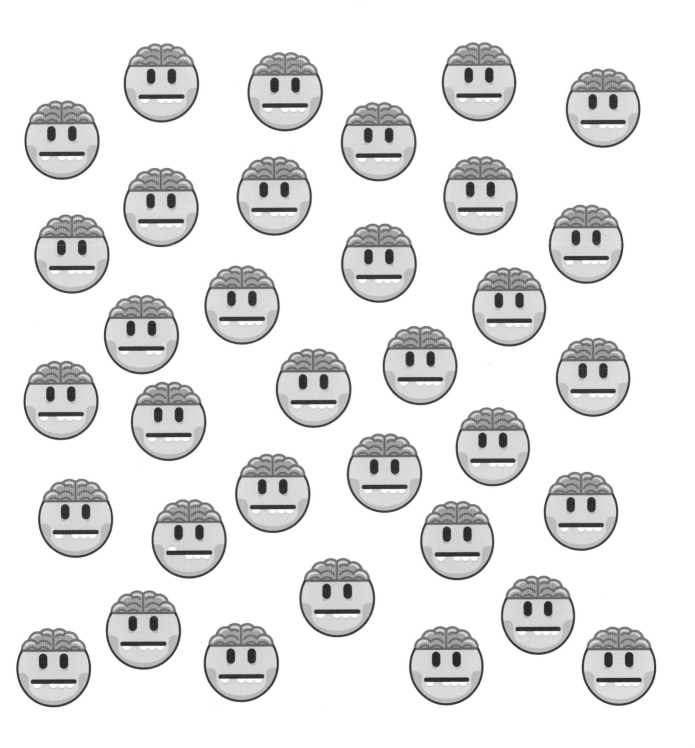

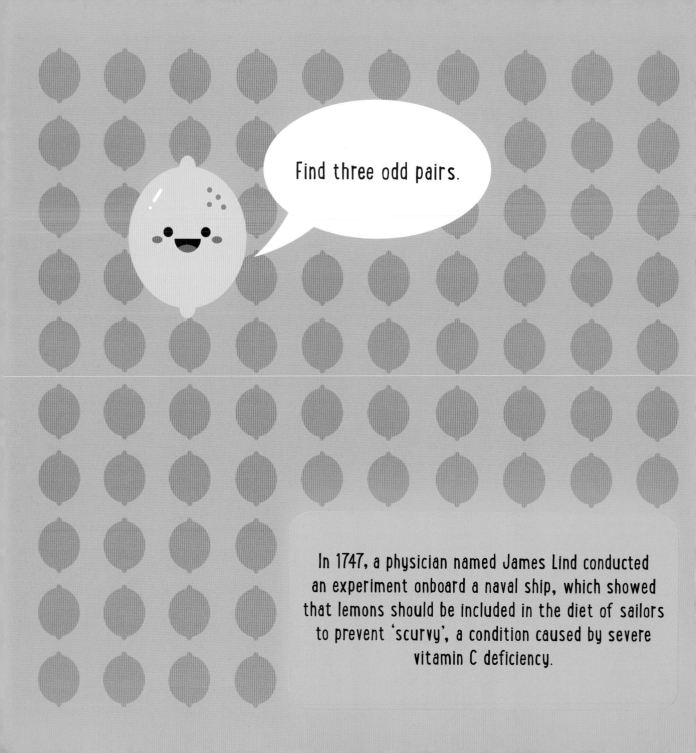

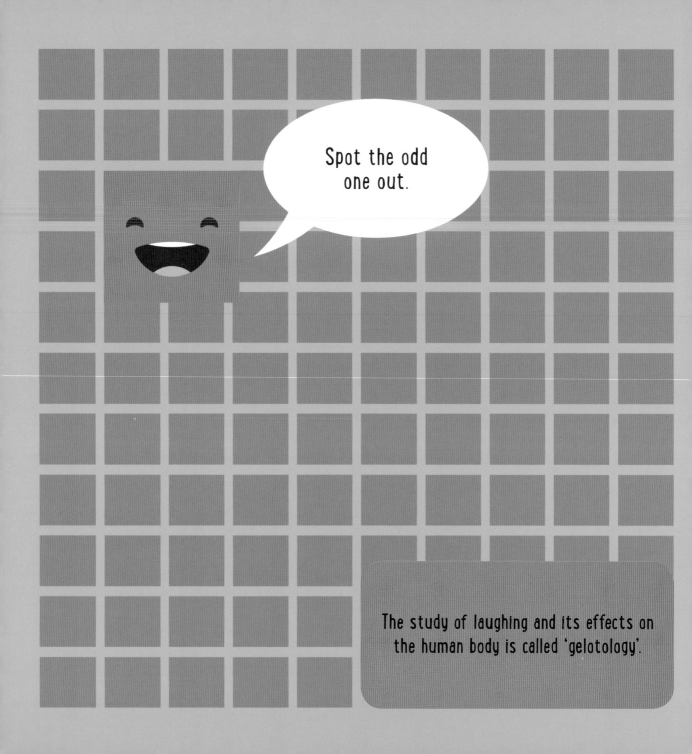

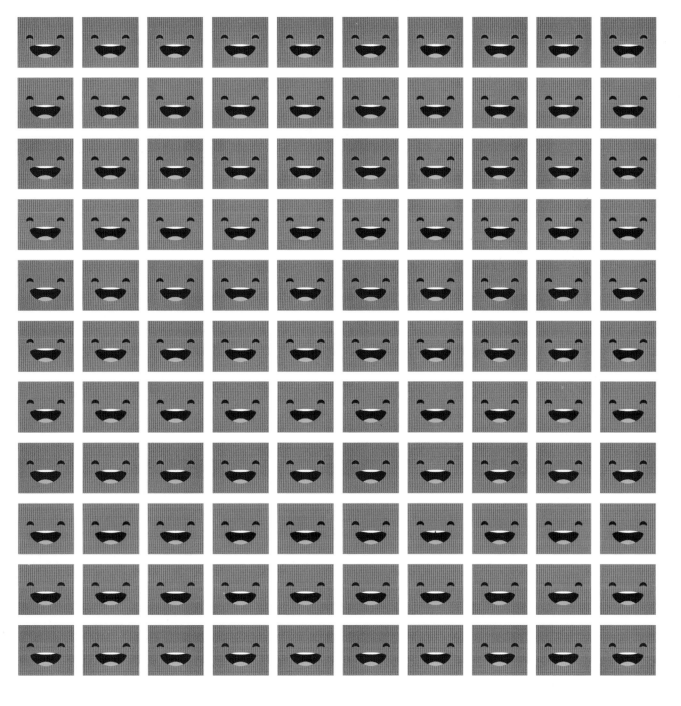

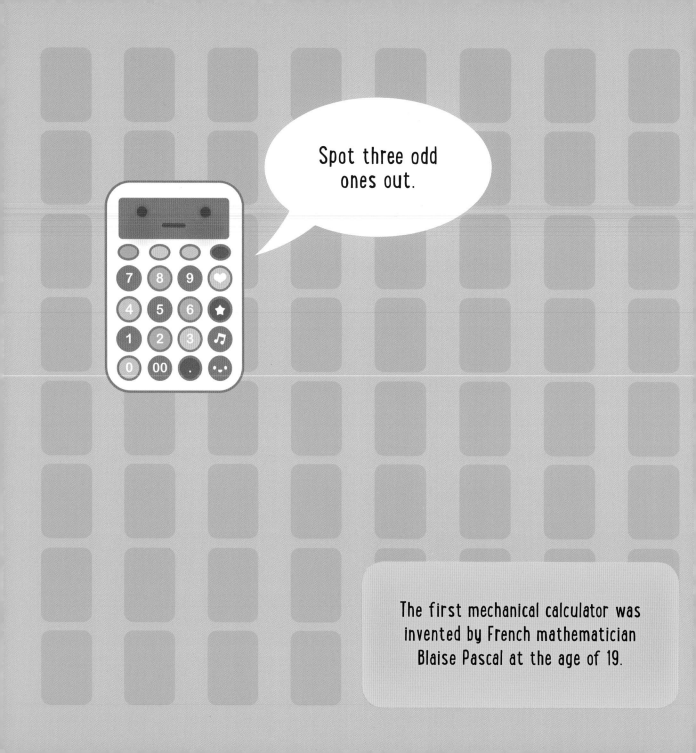

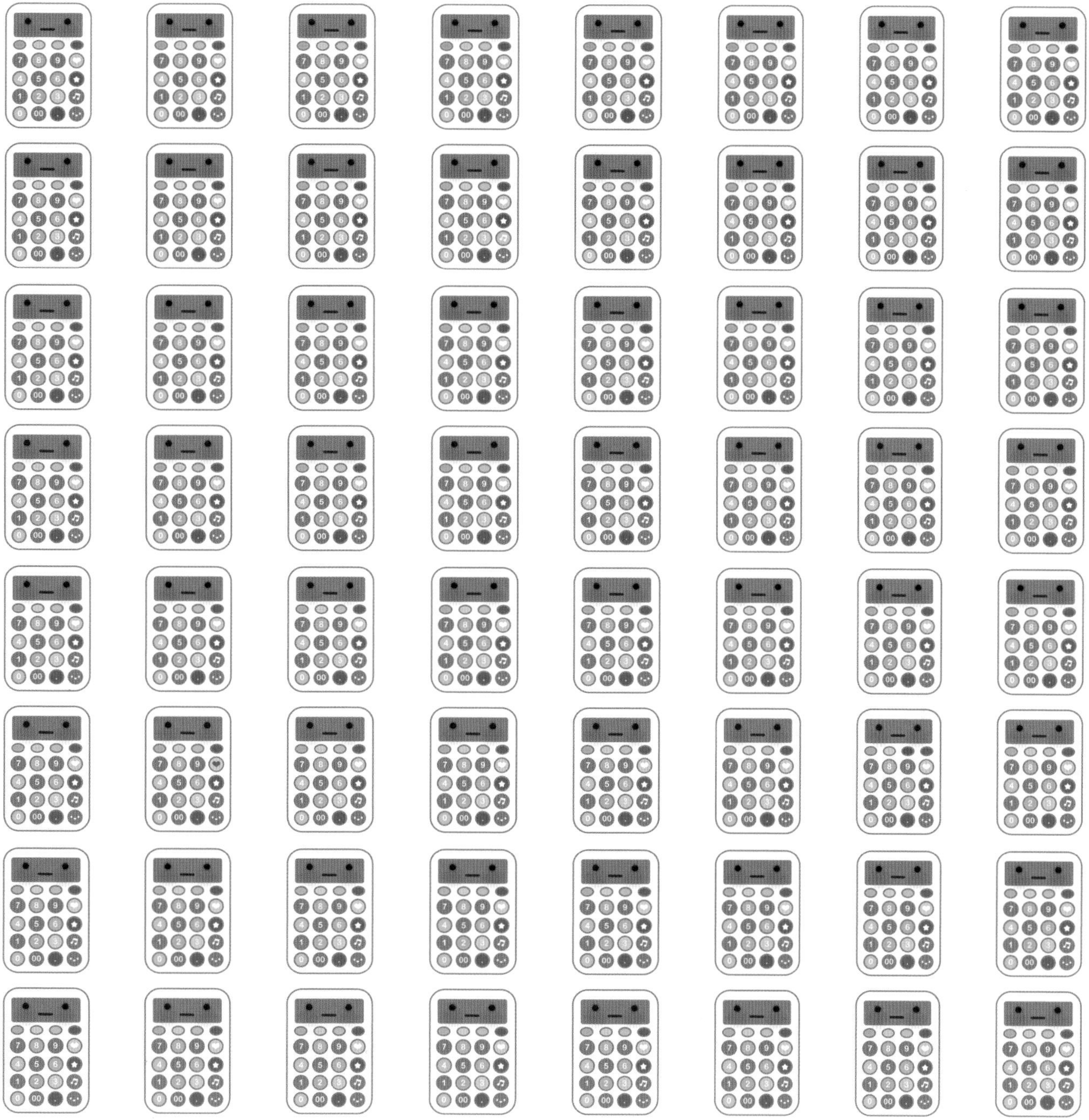

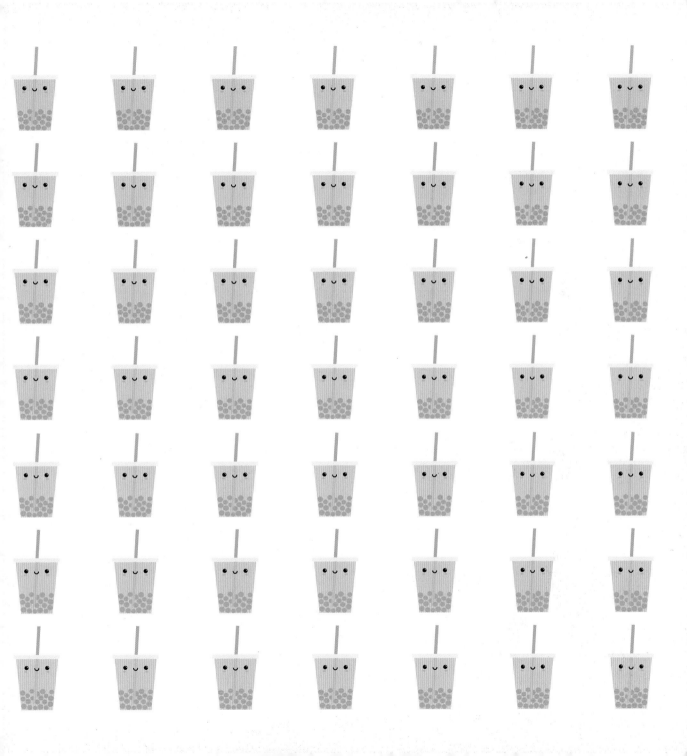

Which milk carton is the largest?

On average, a dairy cow will produce around 200,000 glasses of milk in its lifetime.

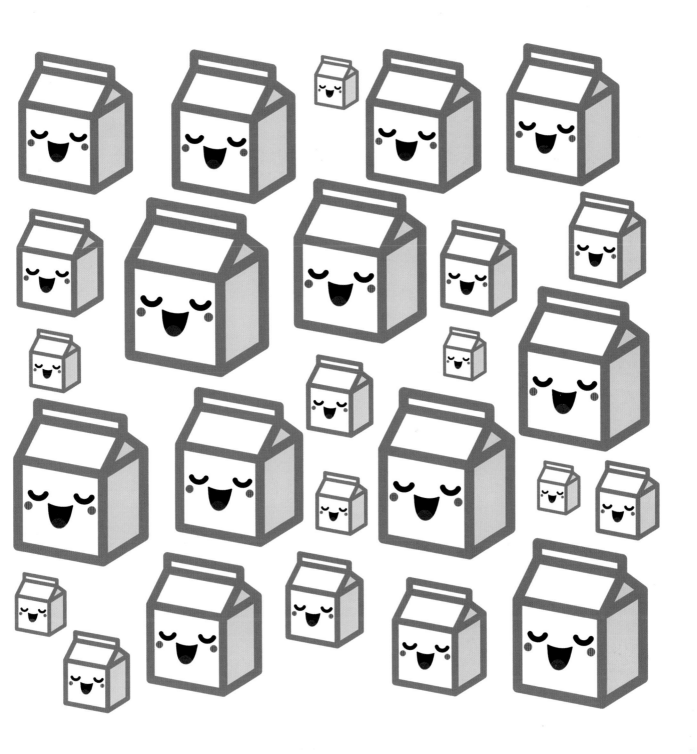

Spot four odd ones out.

This type of plant is called a succulent. Succulent comes from the Latin word 'sucus', meaning juice or sap.

Spot five odd ones out.

The oldest domestic cat on record lived to 34.

All the Answers

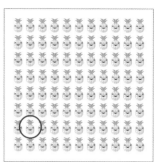

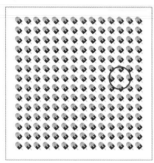

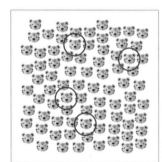

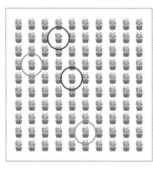

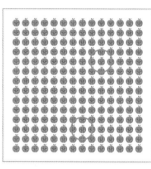

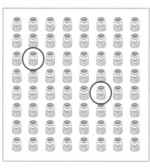

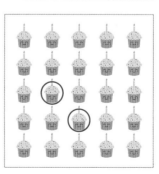

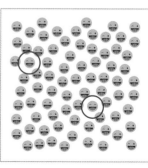

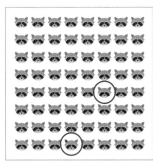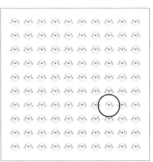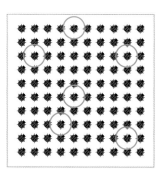
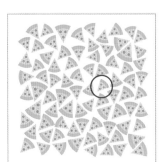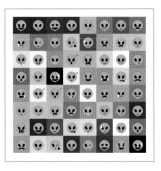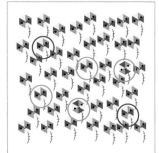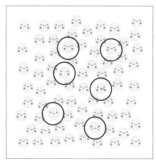
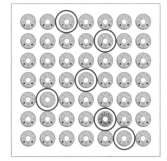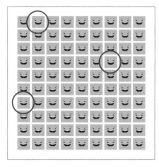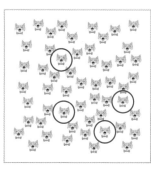
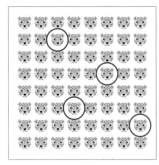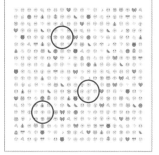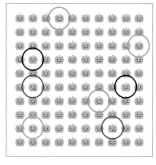

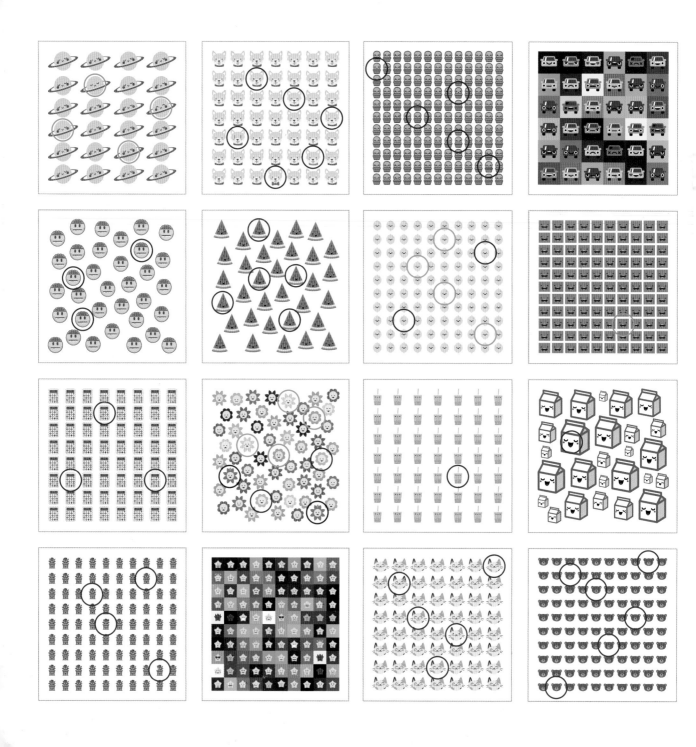